Soups & Stews

tuscan chicken with white beans

1 large fresh fennel bulb (about ¾ pound)
1 teaspoon olive oil
8 ounces boneless skinless chicken thighs, cut into ¾-inch
  pieces
1 teaspoon dried rosemary leaves, crushed
½ teaspoon black pepper
1 can (14½ ounces) no-salt-added stewed tomatoes
1 can (14½ ounces) fat-free reduced-sodium chicken broth
1 can (15 ounces) cannellini beans, rinsed and drained
  Hot pepper sauce (optional)

1. Cut off and reserve ¼ cup chopped feathery fennel tops. Chop bulb into ½-inch pieces. Heat oil in large saucepan over medium heat. Add chopped fennel bulb; cook 5 minutes, stirring occasionally.

2. Sprinkle chicken with rosemary and pepper; add to saucepan. Cook and stir 2 minutes. Add tomatoes and chicken broth; bring to a boil. Cover; simmer 10 minutes. Stir in beans; simmer, uncovered, 15 minutes or until chicken is cooked through and sauce thickens. Season to taste with hot pepper sauce, if desired. Ladle into 4 shallow bowls; top with reserved fennel tops.

Makes 4 servings

tuscan chicken with white beans

creamy carrot soup

3 cups water
4 cups sliced carrots
½ cup chopped onion
2 tablespoons packed brown sugar
2 teaspoons curry powder
2 cloves garlic, minced
⅛ teaspoon ground ginger
   Dash ground cinnamon
½ chicken flavor bouillon cube
½ cup skim milk

In large saucepan, bring water to a boil. Add remaining ingredients except milk. Reduce heat to low; simmer 40 minutes or until carrots are tender. Remove from heat; pour mixture in batches into food processor or blender. Process until smooth. Return mixture to saucepan. Over low heat, stir in milk, heating until warm but not boiling. Serve warm.   *Makes 6 servings*

*Favorite recipe from **The Sugar Association, Inc.***

hearty minestrone

1 cup dried pinto beans
2 teaspoons olive oil
½ cup chopped red onion
1 clove garlic, minced
3 cans (10 ounces each) no-salt-added whole tomatoes, undrained, chopped
1 medium potato, cut into ½-inch cubes
1 cup coarsely chopped carrots
1 cup thinly sliced zucchini
1 to 1¼ cups coarsely shredded cabbage
⅔ cup coarsely chopped leek
½ cup coarsely chopped celery
2 cups no-salt-added vegetable juice cocktail
2 cups water
1 tablespoon chopped fresh basil
1 teaspoon chopped fresh sage
2 bay leaves
¼ teaspoon black pepper
1 cup uncooked small shell pasta
¼ cup freshly grated Parmesan cheese
1 tablespoon chopped fresh parsley

1. Place pinto beans in large glass bowl; cover completely with water. Soak 6 to 8 hours or overnight. Drain beans; discard water.

2. Heat oil in large heavy saucepan or Dutch oven over medium heat. Add onion and garlic; cook and stir until onion is tender. Drain tomatoes, reserving liquid. Add tomatoes to saucepan; mix well. Add pinto beans and vegetables. Stir in vegetable juice, water and reserved tomato liquid. Add basil, sage, bay leaves and black pepper. Bring to a boil over high heat; reduce heat. Cover; simmer 2 hours, stirring occasionally. Add pasta 15 minutes before serving. Cook, uncovered, until soup thickens. Remove bay leaves; discard. Top with Parmesan and parsley.   *Makes 10 (1½-cup) servings*

hearty minestrone

hearty pasta and chick-pea chowder

6 ounces uncooked rotini pasta
2 tablespoons olive oil
¾ cup chopped onion
½ cup thinly sliced carrot
½ cup chopped celery
2 cloves garlic, minced
¼ cup all-purpose flour
1½ teaspoons dried Italian seasoning
⅛ teaspoon red pepper flakes
⅛ teaspoon black pepper
2 cans (14½ ounces each) chicken broth
1 can (19 ounces) chick-peas, rinsed and drained
1 can (14½ ounces) Italian-style stewed tomatoes
6 slices bacon
Grated Parmesan cheese

1. Cook rotini according to package directions. Rinse, drain and set aside.

2. Meanwhile, heat oil in 4-quart Dutch oven over medium-high heat until hot. Add onion, carrot, celery and garlic. Cook and stir over medium heat 5 to 6 minutes or until vegetables are crisp-tender.

3. Remove from heat. Stir in flour, Italian seasoning, red pepper flakes and black pepper until well blended. Gradually stir in broth. Return to heat and bring to a boil, stirring frequently. Boil, stirring constantly, 1 minute. Reduce heat to medium. Stir in cooked pasta, chick-peas and tomatoes. Cook 5 minutes or until heated through.

4. Meanwhile, place bacon between double layer of paper towels on paper plate. Microwave at HIGH 5 to 6 minutes or until bacon is crisp. Drain and crumble.

5. Sprinkle each serving with bacon and grated cheese. Serve immediately.   *Makes 6 servings (about 7 cups)*

hearty pasta and chick-pea chowder

japanese noodle soup

1 package (8½ ounces) Japanese udon noodles
1 teaspoon vegetable oil
1 medium red bell pepper, cut into thin strips
1 medium carrot, diagonally sliced
2 green onions, thinly sliced
2 cans (14½ ounces each) fat-free reduced-sodium beef broth
1 cup water
1 teaspoon reduced-sodium soy sauce
½ teaspoon grated fresh ginger
½ teaspoon black pepper
2 cups thinly sliced fresh shiitake mushrooms, stems removed
4 ounces daikon (Japanese radish), peeled and cut into thin strips
4 ounces firm tofu, drained and cut into ½-inch cubes

1. Cook noodles according to package directions, omitting salt; drain. Rinse; set aside.

2. Heat oil in large nonstick saucepan until hot. Add red bell pepper, carrot and green onions; cook about 3 minutes or until slightly softened. Stir in beef broth, water, soy sauce, ginger and black pepper; bring to a boil. Add mushrooms, daikon and tofu; reduce heat and simmer 5 minutes.

3. Place noodles in soup tureen; ladle soup over noodles.

Makes 6 servings

hearty tortellini soup

1 small red onion, chopped
2 medium carrots, chopped
2 ribs celery, thinly sliced
1 small zucchini, chopped
2 plum tomatoes, chopped
2 cloves garlic, minced
2 cans (14½ ounces each) chicken broth
1 can (15 to 19 ounces) red kidney beans, rinsed and drained
2 tablespoons *French's®* Worcestershire Sauce
1 package (9 ounces) refrigerated tortellini pasta

1. Heat *2 tablespoons oil* in 6-quart saucepot or Dutch oven over medium-high heat. Add vegetables, tomatoes and garlic. Cook and stir 5 minutes or until vegetables are crisp-tender.

2. Add broth, *½ cup water,* beans and Worcestershire. Heat to boiling. Stir in pasta. Return to boiling. Cook 5 minutes or until pasta is tender, stirring occasionally. Serve with crusty bread and grated Parmesan cheese, if desired.   *Makes 4 servings*

Prep Time: 15 minutes
Cook Time: 10 minutes

hearty tortellini soup

hearty vegetable gumbo

Nonstick cooking spray
½ cup chopped onion
½ cup chopped green bell pepper
¼ cup chopped celery
 2 cloves garlic, minced
 2 cans (14½ ounces each) no-salt-added stewed tomatoes
 2 cups no-salt-added tomato juice
 1 can (15 ounces) red beans, rinsed and drained
 1 tablespoon chopped fresh parsley
¼ teaspoon dried oregano leaves
¼ teaspoon hot pepper sauce
 2 bay leaves
1½ cups uncooked quick-cooking brown rice
 1 package (10 ounces) frozen chopped okra, thawed

1. Spray 4-quart Dutch oven with cooking spray; heat over medium heat until hot. Add onion, bell pepper, celery and garlic. Cook and stir 3 minutes or until crisp-tender.

2. Add stewed tomatoes, tomato juice, beans, parsley, oregano, pepper sauce and bay leaves. Bring to a boil over high heat. Add rice. Cover; reduce heat to medium-low. Simmer 15 minutes or until rice is tender.

3. Add okra; cook, covered, 5 minutes more or until okra is tender. Remove and discard bay leaves.   *Makes 4 (2-cup) servings*

hearty vegetable gumbo

country bean soup

1¼ cups dried navy beans or lima beans, rinsed and drained
2½ cups water
¼ pound salt pork or fully cooked ham, chopped
¼ cup chopped onion
½ teaspoon dried oregano leaves
¼ teaspoon salt
¼ teaspoon ground ginger
¼ teaspoon dried sage
¼ teaspoon black pepper
2 cups fat-free (skim) milk
2 tablespoons butter

1. Place navy beans in large saucepan; add enough water to cover beans. Bring to a boil; reduce heat and simmer 2 minutes. Remove from heat; cover and let stand for 1 hour. (Or, cover beans with water and soak overnight.)

2. Drain beans and return to saucepan. Stir in 2½ cups water, salt pork, onion, oregano, salt, ginger, sage and pepper. Bring to a boil; reduce heat. Cover and simmer 2 to 2½ hours or until beans are tender. (If necessary, add more water during cooking.) Add milk and butter, stirring until mixture is heated through and butter is melted. Season with additional salt and pepper, if desired.

Makes 6 servings

country bean soup

cream of broccoli and cheese soup

1 cup chopped onion

3 cloves garlic, minced

3 tablespoons all-purpose flour

4 cans (14½ ounces each) fat-free reduced-sodium chicken
    broth

1½ pounds fresh broccoli, chopped

1½ pounds baking potatoes, peeled and cubed

½ cup fat-free (skim) milk, divided

1 cup (4 ounces) shredded reduced-fat Cheddar cheese

½ teaspoon salt

¼ teaspoon white pepper

    Nonstick cooking spray

    Ground nutmeg (optional)

1. Spray 4-quart Dutch oven or large saucepan with cooking spray; heat over medium heat. Add onion and garlic; cook until tender. Add flour; cook and stir over low heat 1 to 2 minutes.

2. Add chicken broth; bring to a boil. Add broccoli and potatoes; reduce heat and simmer, covered, about 15 minutes or until vegetables are tender. Remove and reserve 1½ cups broccoli mixture with slotted spoon.

3. Process remaining broccoli mixture in batches in food processor or blender until smooth; return to Dutch oven. Stir in reserved broccoli mixture and milk. Cook over medium heat until heated through. Remove from heat; stir in cheese until melted. Stir in salt and pepper. Sprinkle with ground nutmeg, if desired.

Makes 8 servings

cream of broccoli and cheese soup

quick tuscan bean, tomato and spinach soup

2 cans (14½ ounces each) diced tomatoes with onions
1 can (14½ ounces) fat-free reduced-sodium chicken broth
2 teaspoons sugar
2 teaspoons dried basil leaves
¾ teaspoon reduced-sodium Worcestershire sauce
1 can (15 ounces) small white beans, rinsed and drained
3 ounces fresh baby spinach leaves or chopped spinach
    leaves, stems removed
2 teaspoons extra-virgin olive oil

1. Combine tomatoes with juice, chicken broth, sugar, basil and Worcestershire sauce in Dutch oven or large saucepan; bring to a boil over high heat. Reduce heat and simmer, uncovered, 10 minutes.

2. Stir in beans and spinach; cook 5 minutes longer or until spinach is tender.

3. Remove from heat; stir in oil just before serving.

Makes 4 (1½-cup) servings

quick tuscan bean, tomato and spinach soup

texas chili

- 4 tablespoons vegetable oil, divided
- 2 large onions, chopped
- 3 large cloves garlic, minced
- 2 pounds boneless sirloin or round steak, cut into ½-inch cubes
- 1 pound ground beef
- 2 cans (16 ounces each) tomatoes in purée
- 1 can (15 to 19 ounces) red kidney beans, undrained
- ⅓ cup *Frank's® RedHot®* Original Cayenne Pepper Sauce
- ¼ cup chili powder
- 2 tablespoons ground cumin
- 1 tablespoon dried oregano leaves
- ½ teaspoon ground black pepper

1. Heat 1 tablespoon oil in 5-quart saucepan or Dutch oven. Add onions and garlic; cook 5 minutes or until tender. Transfer to small bowl; set aside.

2. Heat remaining 3 tablespoons oil in saucepan. Add sirloin and ground beef in batches; cook about 15 minutes or until well browned. Drain off fat.

3. Stir in remaining ingredients. Bring to a boil over medium-high heat. Return onions and garlic to saucepan. Simmer, partially covered, 1 hour or until meat is tender. Garnish with shredded Cheddar cheese and chopped green onion, if desired.

Makes 10 servings

Prep Time: 15 minutes
Cook Time: 1 hour 20 minutes

white bean and escarole soup

1½ cups dried baby lima beans
1 teaspoon olive oil
½ cup chopped celery
⅓ cup coarsely chopped onion
2 cloves garlic, minced
2 cans (about 10 ounces each) no-salt-added whole
    tomatoes, undrained, chopped
½ cup chopped fresh parsley
2 tablespoons fresh rosemary
¼ teaspoon black pepper
3 cups shredded fresh escarole

1. Place dried lima beans in large glass bowl; cover completely with water. Soak 6 to 8 hours or overnight. Drain beans; place in large saucepan or Dutch oven. Cover beans with about 3 cups water; bring to a boil over high heat. Reduce heat to low. Cover and simmer about 1 hour or until soft. Drain; set aside.

2. Heat oil in small skillet over medium heat. Add celery, onion and garlic; cook and stir 5 minutes or until onion is tender. Remove from heat.

3. Add celery mixture and tomatoes with juice to beans. Stir in parsley, rosemary and pepper. Cover and simmer over low heat 15 minutes. Add escarole; simmer 5 minutes.

Makes 6 (1½-cup) servings

white bean and escarole soup

black bean & pork stew

2 (15-ounce) cans cooked black beans, rinsed and drained

2 cups water

1 pound boneless ham, cut into ¾-inch cubes

¾ pound BOB EVANS® Italian Dinner Link Sausage, cut into 1-inch pieces

¾ pound BOB EVANS® Smoked Sausage, cut into 1-inch pieces

1 pint cherry tomatoes, stems removed

1 medium onion, chopped

1 teaspoon red pepper flakes

6 cloves garlic, minced

⅛ teaspoon grated orange peel

Cornbread or rolls (optional)

Preheat oven to 350°F. Combine all ingredients except cornbread in large Dutch oven. Bring to a boil over high heat, skimming foam off if necessary. Cover; transfer to oven. Bake 30 minutes; uncover and bake 30 minutes more, stirring occasionally. Serve hot with cornbread, if desired, or cool slightly, then cover and refrigerate overnight. Remove any fat from surface. Reheat over low heat. Refrigerate leftovers. *Makes 8 servings*

black bean & pork stew

The publisher would like to thank the companies and organizations listed below for the use of their recipes and photographs in this publication.

Bob Evans®

Reckitt Benckiser Inc.

The Sugar Association, Inc.